GARDEN BIRDS

BIRDS

Richard Allen

ISBN 978-0-9934779-5-9
Jardine Press Ltd 2018
www.jardinepress.co.uk

limited edition prints of the images
in this book are available from the author

for Sally

Contents

Introduction

Introduction

Some of my earliest birdwatching memories are of birds in our small narrow garden in Berkshire. I can still vividly recall the Blackbird singing from our roof gable on a summer's evening, the rows of House Sparrows along the chain-link fence, and the excitement of a Siskin appearing on the orange-netted peanut feeder.

Many people's first experience of watching birds is in their garden. Put up a bird table or a nest box and you enter the world of Robins, Blue Tits and Starlings. It is fascinating to see the daily comings and goings, each species having its own distinctive character and behaviour. Cheeky and acrobatic Great and Blue Tits on the feeders, chattering Sparrows in the bushes, Starlings arriving in a noisy gang, while a Dunnock quietly feeds, unconcerned on the ground.

The cast of characters will change with seasons and the weather. Summer finds Robins, tits and Blackbirds nesting and Swifts screaming around the roof tops, by autumn the Swallows are heading south while finches and tits are forming mixed roving flocks. Winter is often the best time for garden birdwatching, short days mean the birds are very actively feeding and a bit of ice and snow may bring in a rarity such as a Redwing or Fieldfare, possibly even a Hawfinch. Spring and the woodpeckers are drumming and bird song reaches its peak and so the cycle begins again.

There is always something to keep a garden watcher interested.

Richard Allen

Wivenhoe
June 2018

Wren

Troglodytes troglodytes

One of the smallest and commonest birds in Britain, found in all habitats from sea cliffs to high mountains, and of course gardens.

Brown above with a speckled brown breast, often cocking its distinctive short tail, Wrens feed busily amongst ivy and along hedgerows, creeping almost like a mouse in the search for spiders and aphids.

For such a small bird the Wren has an amazingly powerful song, a repeated series of loud trills and ringing notes echoing through the undergrowth. It also has a harsh scolding "zeck" call when danger, such as a cat, approaches.

The male will build several neat, round nests, the females then chooses the one that suits her, and which is then lined with moss and feathers.

Great Spotted Woodpecker

Dendrocopus major

The population of Great Spotted Woodpecker has increased greatly over the last half century and it is now a regular garden visitor. Coming to nut and suet feeders it is an exotically colourful and agile addition to our garden birds.

Boldly patterned black and white, the males have a red patch on the back of the head, whilst young birds in summer have a red crown. Great Spotted Woodpeckers have a distinctive undulating flight, showing large white shoulder patches and calling with a loud "keck....keck".

Great Spotted Woodpeckers start "drumming" (a short, very fast hammering on a favoured deadwood branch) in early spring to advertise that this territory is occupied. Not to be confused with the slower, more methodical taps as they chip out grubs and insects from rotten stumps and branches.

Swift

Apus apus

There is no better indication that summer has finally arrived than a flock of Swifts screaming around the roof tops.

Swifts are a dusky dark brown with a paler throat, they have long scythe shaped wings and a short forked tail. They have short "clinging" feet, used for hanging onto walls or crawling into nesting cavities, no good for perching on wires as swallows and martins do.

Swifts are however masters of the air, in their dynamic aerial lives they feed, sleep and even mate on the wing. When a young Swift leaves the nest in early August and migrates to Southern Africa it will not touch land again until it returns to nest as an adult.

Tawny Owl

Strix aluco

Gardens with a few large trees or bordering woods and parks may be lucky to host Tawny Owls. A widespread medium sized owl with dark eyes, and appearing in two colour phases, a rich tawny brown, and a paler greyer form.

They are as most owls nocturnal, and often the only sighting is of a dark shape flying across a clearing at dusk. Sometimes however a commotion amongst others birds, Blackbirds and Jays in particular, will mean a Tawny Owl has been discover in the open in daylight. The smaller birds will continue to mob the owl until it retreats to its roosting hole.

The familiar "tu-whit, tu-whoo" call of Tawny Owls is in fact two birds duetting, the male has the wavering hoot, while the female calls the sharper "ker-vick".

Pied Wagtail

Motacilla alba

A charming and lively bird, Pied Wagtails can be found on lawns, pavements and roofs chasing insects and constantly wagging its tail. They like to nest in holes in walls, under roof tiles, in sheds and even occasionally on the engines of still operating tractors.

Males are handsomely patterned black and white, while the very similar female has a more sooty grey back. Pied Wagtails are with us all year round, although in winter they lose their black throats and gather in small flocks in search of their insect food. Stream edges, sewage works, playing fields and especially in frosty weather sheltered garden are favoured at this time of year.

Winter is also the time when large flocks of Pied Wagtails will gather at dusk to roost in our towns and cities, taking advantage of the warmer urban environment.

Dunnock

Prunella modularis

This small unobtrusive bird is one of our most common garden visitors; it is often seen quietly shuffling, almost mouse-like, under hedges or at the edge of flower beds. The Dunnock, (from dun, a grey-brown bird), is sometimes called the Hedge Sparrow, but is completely unrelated to House or Tree Sparrows.

Dunnocks are mostly streaked grey and brown, but have a lovely soft blue-grey collar and eye-brow, and a deep red eye when seen well. In spring it has a beautiful thin high pitched warbling song given from the top of a blackthorn bush other small shrub or tree.

Dunnocks are a year round feature of our gardens, parks and woods, but in winter they are joined by Dunnocks from the northern forests of Europe crossing the North Sea to escaping the harsh winter weather.

Robin

Erithacus rubecula

The Robin needs no introduction, its red breast, cheery character and companionship when digging the garden (on the continent they will follow rooting wild boar), has made it a firm favourite with everyone. They are well known for nesting in unusual places, in garden sheds, old teapots, hanging baskets and even under car bonnets.

A much loved songster the Robins clear, beautiful song can be heard in the depth of winter as well as spring and summer as Robin defend a territory throughout the year. They will also sing at night by the light of street lamps or supermarket car park lighting.

Young Robins are very different from adults, they lack the red breast and instead have speckled front and are spotted with buff. They gradually acquire the orange-red colouring and are indistinguishable from adults by autumn.

Swallow

Hirundo rustica

The Swallow is a traditional herald of spring arriving from their South African wintering grounds from early April onwards. It's a long and perilous journey, crossing both the Sahara and the Mediterranean, so it is always a delight to hear the sweet twittering song of a newly arrived Swallow.

Swallows build a cup-shaped mud nest on a beam or ledge in outbuilding, stables and porches, often returning year after year to the same site. They have long tail streamers, a white belly and deep red forehead and throat. Swallows generally fly low, swooping over meadows and lawns to catch their insect prey. House Martins by contrast tend to fly higher, above the roof tops and have a diagnostic white rump patch.

Come late summer and autumn both Swallows and Martins will gather in chattering, excitable flocks on wires and roofs in preparation for the long journey back south.

Blackbird

Turdus merula

The exquisite rich fluty song of the Blackbird is a special treat on an early summer's evening, sung from a chimney pot or aerial and often accompanied by screaming Swifts high overhead.

The Blackbird is a common and well loved garden bird, the male being coal black with a deep orange-yellow bill and eye-ring. The female is a warm brown and has a mottled breast and throat, vaguely reminiscent of a thrush. Earthworms are a favourite food and after a summer shower they can be seen eagerly gathering beakfuls to feed hungry youngsters.

An early nester, Blackbirds can have several broods of young during the spring and summer, often nesting in sheds and amongst tangled ivy. Come winter many of our birds depart for southern climes, being replaced by others from the forests of Eastern Europe escaping the harsh continental winter weather.

Song Thrush

Turdus philomelos

A well loved garden bird, the Song Thrush is sadly declining in numbers for a variety of not fully understood reasons. This is a shame for not only to they consume that gardener's enemy the snail, smashing them against a carefully selected stone anvil, but they are also wonderful songsters.

Starting in early spring, Song Thrushes have a loud and proclaiming song given lustily from the top of a tree or aerial. Infinitely varied, individual phrases are repeated three or four times, distinguishing the song from the slower, more fluty sounds of the Blackbird.

Some Song Thrushes are resident remaining with us all year, others head for southern Europe in autumn, while in winter many birds arrive from the frozen Scandinavian forests.

Sparrowhawk

Accipiter nisus

When I started watching birds Sparrowhawks were a rarity, their numbers decimated by organochlorine pesticides in the 50s and 60s. Since the banning of these chemicals the population has recovered and Sparrowhawks can now regularly be seen hunting gardens, parks and woodlands. I do still get a thrill however everytime I see a Sparrowhawk performing its roller-coaster display flight over a wood in the early spring sunshine.

Most often seen in flight, zipping through gaps in hedges with a distinctive "flap, flap, glide" action, the shorter, rounded wings marking it as different from the similar sized Kestrel. Males are slaty blue-grey above and barred below, and are smaller than the browner females.

The presence of a Sparrowhawk is often betrayed by the alarm calls of small birds hidden deep in cover, and the hawk will be escorted away by a noisy flock of tightly packed Starlings.

Blue Tit

Cyanistes caeruleus

The Blue Tit is a familiar garden bird, a regular diner at bird tables, and is easily encouraged to nest with the provision of a suitable nestbox.

Its small size and the characteristic blue "beret" crown readily distinguish it from the Great Tit. An inquisitive bird, in the past known for pecking open the tops of doorstep milk bottles, and will peck at the putty in window frames.

In late summer and autumn young birds, (which have a yellowish wash over head and wings), and adults will gather into mixed flocks with other tits, Nuthatches and Goldcrests to roam the gardens and woods together. There is safety in numbers, more alert eyes to spot a marauding Sparrowhawk.

Great Tit

Parus major

This is the largest British tit, a frequent visitor to bird feeders, and will readily take to garden nest boxes. Great Tits have a black cap, white cheeks, a yellow breast and belly neatly divided by a black band down the middle, which is wider in males. They are very acrobatic and intelligent birds in the search for food, often seen holding nuts and seeds with their feet as they break into them with their bills.

The Great Tits ringing "teacher, teacher" song is one of the earliest sounds of spring and pairs will take ownership of a nest box or hole from early March onwards. Young birds can be told from adults by their yellowish cheeks, and will join together with other young tits in roving late summer flocks.

Coal Tits, (bottom left on feeder), is another garden visitor in areas with a few pines, often carrying off seeds to cache in crevices or under bark. Smaller than a Great Tit they have a white nape patch, pale grey-buff underparts, and a thin high-pitched call.

Starling

Sturnus vulgaris

The gregarious and engaging Starling is always worth a second look. In fresh plumage it has a slick glossy purple and green sheen to its feathers which have white and buff tips, and a sharp yellow bill. The youngsters, which appear from late May onwards, are a soft grey-brown in colour and gradually attain adult plumage by the autumn.

Starlings nest in holes in trees and buildings, the adults commuting to grasslands to forage for leatherjackets to feed the nestlings. The song is a rich and varied stream of squeaks and whistles incorporating much mimicry of other birds and man-made sounds, (they are closely related to Myna birds).

Come winter the resident birds are joined by thousands of Starlings from across Eastern Europe and Russia. These form huge flocks or "murmurations" as they gather to roost in reed beds or on buildings.

House Sparrow

Passer domesticus

House Sparrows or "spudges" were once among our commonest British birds, a frequent and familiar garden visitor. However over the decades numbers have been drastically reduced, a variety of reasons are to blame, modern farming practises, loss of food source, (motors replacing horses and the loss of spilt oats), and pollution in towns and cities are some quoted.

They do seem to have recovered a bit of late, and the bold "cock-sparrer" can still be found chirping away from privet hedges and guttering, building their untidy nests under eaves and in holes in walls.

Male House Sparrows have a grey crown and black throat, while the females are plainer grey-brown with a buffy cream eye stripe. They are very characterful birds, enjoying a good dust bath, and having a robust courtship with several males chasing a female around with much tail fanning, wing quivering and loud chirruping chatter.

16

Chaffinch *Fringilla coelebs*
Brambling *Fringilla montifringilla*

The Chaffinch, (front bird), is one of Britain commonest breeding birds found in most habitats with a few trees and is a regular year round garden visitor. The male is a fine sight with his blue-grey crown, chestnut back and pinky-orange throat and breast. The female is more sombrely attired mainly in buffs and browns with bold white wing markings. Both sexes have a characteristic sharp "fink" call and the male sings a rapid descending trill.

Rather shy when nesting Chaffinches build a beautifully neat cup-shaped nest in a tree fork camouflaged with lichen and moss.

The Brambling is a close relative of the Chaffinch, but breeds in the extensive birch forests of Fenno-Scandinavia arriving in this country from October onwards. Sometimes appearing in gardens in to feed on beech mast or joining Chaffinches at feeders. Males have a blackish head, while both sexes have a rich orange breast, white belly and an obvious white rump in flight.

17

Goldfinch

Carduelis carduelis

The Goldfinch is a relatively new visitor to gardens where it has taken readily to feeders filled with niger seed or sunflower hearts. These seeds are similar to Goldfinches "wild" food of thistle, teasel and alder; all have small seed which are extracted by the birds fine tweezer-like bill.

With its scarlet face and gold emblazoned wings it is easy to see why in the past the Goldfinch was a popular cage bird. It also features often in art as a symbol of the resurrection, or a the bird who drew a thorn from the crown around Christ's head.

The collective name for Goldfinches is "charm", derived from the 16th century "a blended noise", and reflects the cheery, sweet twittering sound that a flock makes when taking to the wing. In winter these flocks will often join with Siskins and Redpolls to feed in birch and alder trees.

Hawfinch

Coccothraustes coccothraustes

A rare and unmistakable visitor to larger gardens, Hawfinches favour hornbeam, cherry and yew trees and will sometimes come to bird tables.

A large impressive finch with a black mask and throat, buffy chestnut head, grey neck shawl and a big, powerful bill. The last is used to crack open the kernels of cherries, haws and sloes, exerting a force of over 50kg.

Hawfinches are shy and wary birds, flying off quickly when disturbed with a loud, sharp "pix" call and displaying a broad white tip to the tail and white wing flashes.

A scarce breeding bird in old woodland the population is boosted in winter by varying numbers arriving to escape the harsh continental weather.